# THE MINIATURE BOOK OF

# COOKIES

**CRESCENT BOOKS**
New York

Published by Salamander Books Ltd.,
129-137 York Way, London N7 9LG, United Kingdom.

© Salamander Books Ltd., 1991

Recipes and photographs on the following pages are the copyright
of Merehurst Press: 15/16, 29/30, 31/32, 33/34, 43/44, 45/46.

All correspondence concerning the content of this volume
should be addressed to Salamander Books Ltd.

This 1991 edition published by Crescent Books, distributed by
Outlet Book Company, Inc., a Random House Company,
225 Park Avenue South, New York, New York 10003.

Printed and bound in Belgium

**ISBN 0-517-06541-X**

8 7 6 5 4 3 2 1

CREDITS

RECIPES BY: *Pat Alburey, Carole Handslip, Lesley Mackley,
Janice Murfitt and Louise Steele*

PHOTOGRAPHY BY: *Sue Atkinson, Paul Grater and Jon Stewart*

DESIGN BY: *Tim Scott*

TYPESET BY: *Maron Graphics, Wembley*

COLOR SEPARATION BY: *P & W Graphics, Pte. Ltd.*

PRINTED IN BELGIUM BY: *Proost International Book Production,
Turnhout, Belgium*

# $\mathcal{C}$ONTENTS

# $\mathcal{A}$LMOND COFFEE
# SLICES

*1½ cups all-purpose flour*
*¼ cup superfine sugar*
*1 tablespoon instant coffee granules*
*½ cup unsalted butter, chopped*
*¼ cup ground almonds*
*beaten egg to glaze*
*¼ cup sliced almonds*
*1 tablespoon granulated sugar*

*S*ift flour into a bowl; stir in sugar and coffee granules. Cut in butter until mixture resembles bread crumbs. Add ground almonds and lightly form into dough. Press into a buttered jellyroll pan. Brush with beaten egg and sprinkle evenly with sliced almonds and granulated sugar. Bake in an oven preheated to 350F (175C) until golden brown, about 20 minutes. Cool in pan 10 minutes. Cut in 18 fingers and transfer to a wire rack to cool completely. *Makes 18 slices*

# CHOCOLATE HAZELNUT CRESCENTS

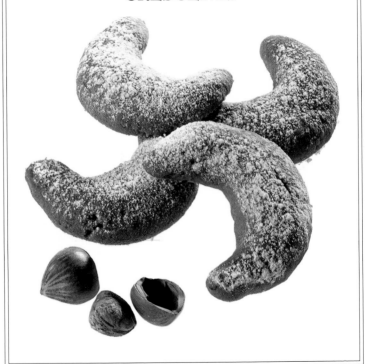

16 tablespoons unsalted butter, softened
⅓ cup sugar
1 egg yolk
1 teaspoon rum
2 cups blanched hazelnuts, ground
about 2 cups all-purpose flour
½ cup cornstarch
2 tablespoons unsweetened cocoa powder
⅓ cup powdered sugar, sifted, to decorate

*I*n a large bowl, beat butter and sugar until light. Beat in egg yolks and rum, then stir in ground nuts. Sift flour, cornstarch and cocoa powder over surface. Using a metal spoon, lightly fold in, adding a little more flour, if necessary, to make a firm dough. Break off small walnut-size pieces. With lightly floured hands, roll each to a 3-inch length, tapering at both ends. Shape in crescents and place on a buttered baking sheet; several will be needed. Bake in an oven preheated to 350F (175C) until firm, about 20-25 minutes. Cool on wire racks. Sift powdered sugar over to coat. *Makes 40 crescents*

# $\mathscr{N}$UTTY
## SHORTBREAD RINGS

½ cup unsalted butter, softened
2 tablespoons superfine sugar
1 small egg yolk
1½ teaspoons instant coffee granules dissolved in
1 teaspoon hot water
1½ teaspoons brandy
¼ cup cornstarch, sifted
1¼ cups all-purpose flour, sifted
⅔ cup walnut halves, coarsely ground
1-2 tablespoons strong coffee
¾ cup powdered sugar, sifted

*I*n a bowl, beat butter and powdered sugar until light. Beat in egg yolk, then coffee and brandy. Sift flour and cornstarch over the surface, then lightly fold in with the ground almonds to make a firm dough. Divide into 16 pieces. On a lightly floured surface, roll each piece to a 7-inch length then form in a circle, pressing the ends firmly together. Place slightly apart on baking sheets, then bake in an oven preheated to 325F (160C) until firm, 20 minutes. Cool on a wire rack. Lightly brush each ring with coffee, then thickly sprinkle with powdered sugar. *Makes 16 rings*

# $\mathcal{P}$EANUT BUTTER COOKIES

½ cup margarine, softened
½ cup crunchy peanut butter
½ cup granulated sugar
¾ cup light-brown sugar
1 egg, beaten
1½ cups all-purpose flour
½ teaspoon baking powder
¾ teaspoon baking soda
½ teaspoon mixed spice
¼ teaspoon ground cinnamon
2 good pinches freshly grated nutmeg
glacé cherry halves and blanched almonds, to decorate

*I*n a bowl, beat margarine, peanut butter, sugars and egg until evenly mixed. Sift flour, baking powder, baking soda and spices over surface, then lightly fold in until evenly combined. Divide off into 25 balls. Place, spaced well apart, on 2 greased baking sheets; flatten to 2-inch circles. Place almonds in center of 12 cookies, glacé cherry halves in center of remaining 13. Refrigerate 30 minutes. Bake in an oven preheated to 375F (190C) until cooked through but not hard, 10-12 minutes. Cool on baking sheets 5 minutes, then transfer to a wire rack to cool completely. *Makes 25 cookies*

# $\mathscr{P}$ECAN & CHOCOLATE CHIP COOKIES

8 tablespoons unsalted butter, softened
¼ cup granulated sugar
⅓ cup packed light-brown sugar
1 egg
1 teaspoon vanilla extract
1 cup all-purpose flour
2 tablespoons unsweetened cocoa powder
½ teaspoon baking soda
½ cup chocolate pieces (4 oz)
½ cup pecans, coarsely chopped

*I*n a bowl, beat together butter and sugars until light. Gradually beat in egg and vanilla. Sift flour, cocoa and baking powder over surface, then fold in lightly with the nuts and chocolate pieces. Place spoonfuls of mixture, spaced well apart, on 2 or 3 greased baking sheets. Bake in an oven preheated to 350F (175C) until beginning to feel firm, 10-15 minutes. Carefully transfer to wire racks to cool and become crisp. Store in an airtight container. *Makes about 28 cookies*

# COFFEE MACAROONS

*1¼ cups ground almonds, sifted*
*½ cup superfine sugar*
*1 tablespoon ground rice or cornstarch*
*1 tablespoon instant coffee granules*
*2 egg whites*
*3 (1 oz) squares semisweet chocolate, chopped*

*I*n a bowl, combine ground almonds, sugar, ground rice and coffee granules. In a bowl, whip egg whites until soft peaks form; gently fold into nut mixture until evenly blended. Roll in 18 small walnut-size balls and place on baking sheets lined with rice paper; press lightly to flatten. Bake in an oven preheated to 300F (150C) until golden, 25-30 minutes. Cool on baking sheets. When cold, peel away surplus rice paper. In a small bowl placed over a saucepan of simmering water, melt chocolate, stirring until smooth. Spread over ½ top of each macaroon. *Makes 18 macaroons*

# CANNOLI

1½ cups all-purpose flour
2 tablespoons powdered sugar
2 tablespoons unsalted butter
2 tablespoons sweet sherry
vegetable oil for deep-frying
10 oz mascarpone cheese
⅓ cup powdered sugar, sifted
¼ cup chopped pistachios
⅓ cup chopped glacé fruits
sifted powdered sugar, to decorate

*F*or the pastry, sift flour and powdered sugar into a bowl. Cut in butter until mixture resembles bread crumbs. Stir in sherry to make a firm dough. Knead lightly, cover and refrigerate 30 minutes. On a lightly floured surface, roll out pastry as thinly as possible. Cut out 14 (3½-inch) squares. Wrap squares around buttered cream horn molds, forming cones. Moisten and seal edges. Deep fry in hot oil until crisp and golden, 1-2 minutes. Drain on paper towels. Carefully remove molds and let stand until completely cold. For the filling, in a bowl, beat together mascarpone, powdered sugar, nuts and fruits. Spoon into cannoli. Dust with powdered sugar. *Makes 14 cannoli*

# $\mathcal{V}$IENNESE COOKIES

1 cup plus 2 tablespoons all-purpose flour
2 tablespoons cocoa powder
½ cup unsalted butter, softened
⅓ cup powdered sugar, sifted
3½ g (1 oz) squares semisweet chocolate, melted
¼ cup unsalted butter, softened
1 cup powdered sugar, sifted
2 teaspoons strong coffee
2 teaspoons milk
powdered sugar and chopped nuts to finish

*I*n a bowl, beat butter and powdered sugar until light. Sift flour and cocoa over surface, then work in to make a smooth piping consistency. Spoon into a pastry bag fitted with a 1-inch fluted nozzle. Pipe 1–½-inch lengths on greased baking sheets, spacing lightly apart. Bake in an oven preheated to 350F (175C) until firm, 15 minutes. Cool on baking sheets several minutes, then transfer to a wire rack to cool completely. Dip cookies in melted chocolate and leave to set. For the butter icing, in a bowl, beat butter with ½ powdered sugar until evenly mixed, then beat in remaining sugar, coffee and milk. Sandwich cookies together. Sprinkle with powdered sugar or chopped nuts. *Makes about 15 cookies*

# $\mathcal{P}$INEAPPLE-GINGER FLORENTINES

6 tablespoons unsalted butter
¼ cup corn syrup
¼ cup all-purpose flour, sifted
1 oz angelica, coarsely chopped
¼ cup crystallized ginger, coarsely chopped
½ cup sliced almonds, coarsely chopped
⅓ cup glacé pineapple, coarsely chopped
1 teaspoon lemon juice
4 oz semisweet chocolate, melted

*I*n a medium-size saucepan, melt butter and corn syrup, then stir in flour, ginger, angelica, almonds, glacé pineapple and lemon juice. Place walnut-sized mounds well apart on 2 baking sheets lined with parchment paper; flatten with a fork. Bake in an oven preheated to 350F (175C) 8-10 minutes. Cool 1 minute, then transfer to a wire rack to cool completely. Spread chocolate over bottom of each cookie. Place chocolate side-up, on a wire rack and mark chocolate in lines with a small palette knife. Let stand until set. *Makes about 14 florentines*

# CRÈME DE MENTHE COOKIES

8 (1-oz) squares semisweet chocolate, chopped
2 tablespoons butter
2 cups graham cracker crumbs
¾ cup plain cake crumbs
superfine sugar
mint sprigs to decorate

FILLING:
¼ cup unsalted butter
¾ cup powdered sugar, sieved
2 teaspoons Crème de Menthe

For the filling, in a bowl, beat butter until soft and smooth. Gradually beat in powdered sugar and Crème de Menthe until light and fluffy. In a bowl set over a saucepan of hot water, melt chocolate and butter stirring occasionally until smooth. Stir in graham cracker and cake crumbs until evenly mixed and mixture forms a ball. On a 10-inch square of foil sprinkled with superfine sugar, roll out chocolate mixture to an 8-inch square. Spread filling evenly over chocolate mixture leaving a ½-inch border. From long edge, roll up carefully in a smooth roll using foil. Wrap in foil and refrigerate until firm. To serve, cut in thin slices and decorate with mint sprigs. *Makes 20 servings*

# $\mathcal{S}$COTTISH
# SHORTBREAD

*½ cup butter, softened*
*5 teaspoons sugar*
*1¼ cups all-purpose flour*
*pinch of salt*
*2 tablespoons fine semolina*
*superfine sugar for sprinkling*

*I*n a medium-size bowl, beat butter with sugar until creamy. Sift in flour and salt, and add semolina. Stir in with a spoon then mix using your hand to a soft dough. On a floured surface knead lightly until smooth. Roll out to a smooth 6-inch diameter circle. Very lightly flour a 7-inch shortbread mold. Place shortbread smooth-side down in mold and press out to fit mold exactly. Very carefully unmold shortbread onto an ungreased baking sheet. Refrigerate 1 hour. If you do not have a shortbread mold, shape dough into a neat circle then place on baking sheet. Prick well with a fork and pinch edge to decorate. Refrigerate 1 hour. Bake in an oven preheated to 325F (165C) until cooked through but still pale, about 35 minutes. As soon as shortbread is removed from oven, sprinkle very lightly with superfine sugar. Cool on baking sheet about 20 minutes then carefully remove to a wire rack. *Makes one (7-inch) shortbread*

# $\mathcal{G}$INGERBREAD
## MEN

4 cups all-purpose flour
pinch of salt
2 teaspoons ground ginger
1 teaspoon ground allspice
2 teaspoons baking soda
2 tablespoons light corn syrup
1/4 cup molasses
1/3 cup packed brown sugar
1/4 cup sugar
1/2 cup butter
1 egg, beaten

*S*ift dry ingredients into a large bowl; form a well in the center. In a medium-size saucepan over moderate heat, combine corn syrup, molasses, sugar and butter until evenly blended. Pour into well, add egg and stir to form a dough. On a lightly floured surface, knead lightly until smooth. Roll out to 1/8-inch thick. Using a gingerbread man cookie cutter, cut out men from the dough. Knead and reroll trimmings until all dough is used. Transfer men to buttered baking sheets. Bake in an oven preheated to 350F (175C) 10-12 minutes. Cool on baking sheets, then remove to wire racks. Leave plain or decorate as desired. *Makes about 24 gingerbread men*

# $\mathcal{A}$MARETTI

*1⅔ cups (6 oz) ground almonds*
*1½ cups powdered sugar, sifted*
*1 egg white*
*2 teaspoons Amaretto*
*a few drops almond extract*
*sifted powdered sugar for sprinkling*

*I*n a large bowl, stir together almonds and sugar; make well in center. In a small bowl, very lightly beat together egg white, Amaretto and almond extract. Pour mixture into well and mix to paste. Shape into 36 equal-size balls and place on baking sheets lined with parchment or waxed paper. Bake in an oven preheated to 350F (175C), until just lightly browned, about 15 minutes. As soon as cookies are removed from oven, sprinkle with powdered sugar. Cool on baking sheets. *Makes about 36 Amaretti*

NOTE: Amaretti can be served at the end of a meal with coffee or as an accompaniment to desserts.

# $\mathcal{A}$DVENT COOKIES

1¼ cups all-purpose flour
⅓ cup butter, chopped
2 tablespoons plus 2 teaspoons superfine sugar
¼ cup ground almonds
1 egg yolk
cold water
1 egg white
1½ cups powdered sugar, sifted
Red, green, yellow, and black food coloring pens
assorted colors fine ribbon

*S*ift flour into a bowl and cut in butter finely. Stir in sugar, ground almonds and egg yolk and enough water to make a soft dough. On a lightly floured surface, knead lightly. Roll out thinly. Using 2¼-inch cutters, cut into shapes. Transfer to 2 lightly floured baking sheets. Make a hole in top of each shape. Bake in an oven pre-heated to 350F (175C) until lightly browned at edges, 10-15 minutes. Cool on a wire rack. For the decoration, in a bowl, combine egg white with sufficient sugar until thick. Beat until glossy. Coat cookies. Leave to set. Using food coloring pens, decorate cookies. Thread a ribbon through each hole at top of cookie. *Makes 24 cookies*

# CHEESE STRAWS

2 cups all-purpose flour
½ teaspoon salt
½ teaspoon cayenne pepper
½ teaspoon dry mustard
½ cup butter, chopped
1 cup shredded Cheddar cheese (4 oz)
1 egg, beaten
FLAVORINGS:
1 tablespoon plus 1 teaspoon finely chopped bell peppers
1 tablespoon plus 1 teaspoon chopped fresh parsley
1 clove garlic, crushed
1 tablespoon plus 1 teaspoon chopped fresh basil

*S*ift flour, salt, cayenne and mustard into a bowl. Cut in butter finely. Stir in cheese and egg to form a dough. On a lightly floured surface, knead until smooth. Cut in 4 pieces. Lightly knead flavorings into separate pieces. Separately, roll out each piece to a large strip 4-inches wide and ¼-inch thick. Cut into ¼-inch wide small strips. Place on buttered baking sheets. Cut trimmings using a 2-inch and a 1½-inch cutter, into rings. Place on baking sheets. Bake in an oven preheated to 400F (205C) until golden, 5-8 minutes. Cool on wire racks. Serve in bundles threaded through rings. *Makes 100 straws*

# CHEESE THINS

1 cup all-purpose flour
½ teaspoon salt
½ teaspoon pepper
½ teaspoon dry mustard
½ cup butter, chopped
1 cup shredded Cheddar cheese (4 oz)
1 tablespoon plus 1 teaspoon regular oats
1 teaspoon cayenne pepper
1 egg white
fennel sprigs to garnish

*S*ift flour, salt, pepper and mustard into a bowl. Cut in the butter finely until the mixture begins to cling together. Using a fork, stir in cheese; mix to a soft dough. On a lightly floured surface, knead gently. Cover and refrigerate 30 minutes. Roll out dough very thinly. Using a 1-inch oval cutter, cut out 80 oval shapes. Arrange on greased baking sheets, spacing apart. Lightly knead trimmings together and re-roll, as necessary. In a small bowl, mix oatmeal and cayenne. Brush each oval with egg white and sprinkle with oatmeal mixture. Bake in an oven preheated to 425F (220C) 5-6 minutes. Cool on baking sheets a few minutes, then, using a palette knife, remove carefully. Serve garnished with fennel sprigs. *Makes 80 pieces*

# $\mathcal{S}$AVORY PINWHEELS

2¼ cups all-purpose flour
½ teaspoon salt
½ teaspoon cayenne pepper
1 teaspoon dry mustard
¾ cup butter, chopped
1 cup shredded Cheddar cheese (4 oz)
1 egg, beaten
parsley sprigs to garnish
1 teaspoon sesame seeds
1 teaspoon poppy seeds
1 teaspoon curry paste
2 teaspoons tomato paste

*S*ift flour, salt, cayenne and mustard into a bowl. Cut in the butter finely. Using a fork, stir in cheese and egg to form a dough. Knead until smooth. Cut in 4. Knead sesame seeds into 1 piece and poppy seeds into another. Form both in 6-inch rolls. Roll remaining 2 pieces of pastry in 8- × 6-inch rectangles. Spread with curry or tomato paste. Roll up and wrap separately in plastic wrap. Refrigerate until firm. Unwrap rolls. Slice thinly and arrange a little apart on baking sheets lined with parchment paper. Bake in an oven preheated to 400F (205C), 6-8 minutes. Cool, then transfer to wire racks. *Makes 96 pieces*

# $\mathcal{W}$ATER CRACKERS

1½ cups all-purpose flour
½ teaspoon salt
1 teaspoon baking powder
3 tablespoons butter, softened
4 tablespoons water
cheese or pâté to serve

*S*ift flour, salt and baking powder into a medium-size bowl; cut in butter until mixture resembles fine bread crumbs. Stir in water to form a dough. On a floured surface, knead dough until smooth. Roll out very thinly. Using 3½-inch round cookie cutter, cut out circles and place on greased baking sheets; prick all over. Knead and re-roll trimmings and cut out more circles until dough is used up. Bake in an oven preheated to 350F (175C) until well cooked and only slightly browned, about 15 minutes. Cool on wire racks. Serve with cheese or pâté. *Makes about 20 cookies*

# $\mathscr{S}$COTTISH
## OATCAKES

*1 cup rolled oats*
*½ teaspoon baking powder*
*pinch of salt*
*2 tablespoons butter, softened*
*2 tablespoons boiling water*

*I*n a bowl, mix together rolled oats, baking powder and salt; cut in butter until mixture resembles coarse bread crumbs. Stir in boiling water to form a sticky dough. Knead until dough becomes drier and smoother. On a lightly floured surface roll out dough to a circle about 8-inches in diameter. Using a plate as a guide, cut dough in a neat circle. Cut 8 equal-size triangles. Over medium heat, heat a griddle; grease very lightly. Cook oatcakes on griddle until cooked through and corners curl up, 8-10 minutes. Cool on a wire rack. Serve with butter and jam. Alternatively, serve with cheese or pâté and relishes. *Makes 8 oatcakes*